Learning About Aquarium Fish

Steven James Petruccio

DOVER PUBLICATIONS, INC.
Mineola, New York

Bibliographical Note

Learning About Aquarium Fish is a new work, first published by Dover Publications, Inc., in 1997.

International Standard Book Number: 0-486-29527-3

Manufactured in the United States of America
Dover Publications, Inc., 31 East 2nd Street, Mineola, N.Y. 11501

Introduction

Fish are very popular pets that are very easy to keep. They have many colors, sizes and shapes, for there are many different kinds in the seas and rivers. Read about the twelve different fish here, then place the stickers in the spaces provided so that each one matches the right description. Soon you will be on your way to starting your own aquarium! Ask at a pet store what to feed your fish.

Angelfish

So thin it seems to disappear when
seen from the front, the angelfish can
be as long as six inches and as tall as
ten. It has bright red eyes, long fins
and a tail with two points. Silver or
blue, the angelfish sometimes re-
mains very still, almost motionless,
in its aquarium. Sea angelfish are
highly colorful—some change their
brilliant colors as they grow older!

Spotted Goldfish

Not all aquarium goldfish are gold. Several varieties of goldfish that probably would not have survived in the wild now exist in many colors with spots and stripes. Some examples are the veilteil, the lionhead, the eggfish, the comet, the meteor, the telescope and the spotted goldfish.

Neon Tetra

In the dim light of an aquarium, the bluish-green stripe on the back of the neon tetra will glow like a neon sign. Shiny and scaly, this fish is generally about two inches long. Though discovered only sixty years ago in the Amazon, the neon tetra is already one of the most common tropical fish to be kept as pets because it is very peaceful.

Molly

Usually black, the molly eats plants and ranges in size from two to five inches. This tropical fish is distinguished by a curved tail and a large back fin, which the male molly likes to display before battle or when showing off to his mate. Mollies are found in the rivers of Central America and North America.

Swordtail

A member of the carp family just like the goldfish, the swordtail is a freshwater fish from Mexico and Central America. It has an enormous tail fin and comes in a variety of colors, most commonly yellow or orange. The female swordtail can grow as large as five inches long, while the male will reach three-and-a-quarter inches and is notable for its ability to swim backwards.

Egyptian Mouthbreeder

The Egyptian mouthbreeder is a scaly African fish with a large back fin and a small, fan-shaped tail. It is often found in the Nile River. Ideal for the aquarium because it gets along so well with other fish, the Egyptian mouthbreeder can be purple, gold, blue or green and not longer than three inches. The female lays her eggs in sand.

Paradise Fish

The paradise fish comes from the rice paddies of Asia. It has wide, sweeping fins and tail, and can be green, yellow, black, blue or white with stripes running down its sides. Paradise-fish eggs are borne in a nest of bubbles that rises to the water's surface. Not longer than three and a half inches, the paradise fish likes floating plants—but not other fish: it is a fighter.

Goldfish

The most common of aquarium fish, the goldfish, a member of the carp family, has been kept as a pet by the Chinese for centuries. Outdoors, goldfish can weigh as much as ten pounds. Aquarium goldfish are never more than several inches long, very easy to breed and can live for as long as twenty-five years!

Cherry Barb

The cherry barb can produce as many as two hundred and fifty babies in one season, and is a good fish with which to start an aquarium. Originally found in the streams of Sri Lanka, this scaly, bright red fish, no bigger than two inches long, likes to hide among the plants of its tank.

Red Betta

Also known as the "Siamese fighting fish," the red betta comes from Singapore and Thailand. Two and a half inches in length, the red betta has a curved tail fin, which is somewhat larger in males than in females. Male red bettas often fight one another, and are notable for butting their heads together angrily.

Blue Gourami

From the island of Sumatra, the blue gourami is a tropical fish that can grow as long as one foot. Gouramis rise to the tank surface to feed and take in air through the gills. They are also popular pet fish because of their habit of joining lips with one another in an act of "kissing"—though no one knows if it shows liking or dislike!

Black Tetra

The black tetra (also known as the "black widow") comes from the rivers of South America. It can be yellow, silver, gray or black with dark vertical bands, and is never longer than two inches. In aquariums, it sometimes develops long fins. In freshwater, black tetras travel together in large groups, called shoals, which move about like a small army.